GOALKEEPERS

AUDREY STEWART

childsworld.com

Published by The Child's World®
800-599-READ • childsworld.com

Copyright © 2025 by The Child's World®
All rights reserved. No part of this book may be reproduced or utilized in any form or by any means without written permission from the publisher.

Photography Credits
Cover: ©AlexeyVS/Getty Images; ©Andy Lyons/Getty Images; page 4: ©irin-k/Shutterstock; page 5: ©Brad Smith/ISI Photos/USSF/Getty Images; page 6: ©Dan Mullan/Getty Images; page 7: ©Jan Kruger/Getty Images; page 9: ©Laurence Griffiths/Getty Images; ©Robert Cianflone/Getty Images; page 10: ©Gene Sweeney Jr./Getty Images; page 11: ©Jamie McDonald/Getty Images; page 13: ©Evening Standard/Getty Images; page 14: ©Rich Lam/Getty Images; page 15: ©Ronald Martinez/Getty Images; page 16: ©Ben Radford/Getty Images; page 17: ©Ivcandy/Getty Images; ©nmvector/Shutterstock; ©Kevin C. Cox/Getty Images; page 18: ©Dean Mouhtaropoulos/Getty Images; page 19: ©Michael Regan/The FA/Getty Images; page 21: ©Visionhaus/Getty Images; page 22: ©Bradley Kanaris/Getty Images; page 25: ©Gaulter Fatia/Getty Images; page 26: ©Valerio Pennicino/Getty Images; page 28: ©Ronald Martinez/Getty Images; page 29: ©Phil Cole/Getty Images

ISBN Information
ISBN 9781503894280 (Reinforced Library Binding)
ISBN 9781503895218 (Portable Document Format)
ISBN 9781503896031 (Online Multi-user eBook)
ISBN 9781503896857 (Electronic Publication)

LCCN
2024942884

Printed in the United States of America

ABOUT THE AUTHOR

Audrey Stewart is a writer, educator, and librarian who has a strong belief that stories have the power to open our minds and connect us all. She writes nonfiction, including a children's series about her years of rescuing stray animals. She lives in San Antonio, Texas, with her husband and their four rescued critters.

CONTENTS

CHAPTER ONE
THE SHOOT-OUT 4

CHAPTER TWO
DEFENDING THE NET 6

CHAPTER THREE
GOALKEEPING LEGENDS 12

CHAPTER FOUR
TODAY'S STAR KEEPERS 18

CHAPTER FIVE
RISING YOUNG STARS 24

Glossary . . . 30
Fast Facts . . . 31
One Stride Further . . . 31
Find Out More . . . 32
Index . . . 32

CHAPTER ONE
THE SHOOT-OUT

The United States Women's National Team (USWNT) was playing Sweden in the 2023 Fédération Internationale de Football Association (**FIFA**) World Cup Round of 16 match. The USWNT was hoping to win their fifth World Cup title, but they couldn't get the ball past Swedish goalkeeper Zećira Mušović. The US had 11 **shots on goal**. Mušović saved every one of them. After 120 minutes of play, including **overtime**, the game was tied 0–0. The winner would be decided in a **penalty shoot-out**.

A penalty shoot-out happens when a soccer game is tied at the end of regular time and overtime. In tournaments and other important games, the score cannot end in a tie. Each team gets at least five shots, and players take turns shooting. The team with the most goals wins the game. Players can shoot left, right, or straight down the middle. In a split second, the goalkeeper has to commit to a direction. In this match, the final **penalty kick** from USWNT player Kelley O'Hara did not go in. Sweden's Lena Hurtig made the next shot, and Sweden won 5–4.

Zećira Mušović allowed only four goals in seven games during the 2023 Women's World Cup. In three of the games, she did not allow the other team to score at all.

CHAPTER TWO
DEFENDING THE NET

Also known as the goalie or keeper, goalkeepers are tough, quick, and brave. They have special rules that only apply to the goalkeeping position. One big difference is that goalies are allowed to use their hands inside the goal area. No other player on the field can use their hands, or the whistle is blown for a **handball**.

During a penalty shoot-out, the goalie is the only player allowed to defend the net.

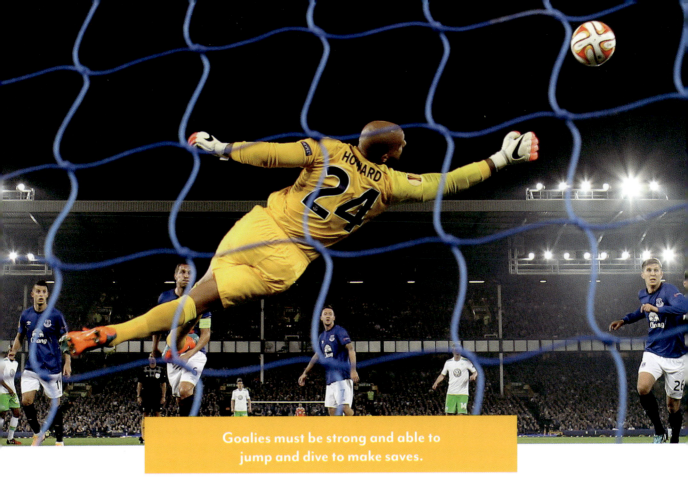

Goalies must be strong and able to jump and dive to make saves.

The job of a goalkeeper is to make sure the other team doesn't score. Goalkeepers have to use their skills to block the ball from crossing the goal line. Some of these skills include quick footwork, diving to both sides, jumping high, and using their arms and hands to block the ball. If a shot gets past the goalkeeper and the other team scores, the goalkeeper has to shake it off and refocus quickly. Goalkeepers must have a level of mental toughness that other players may not have. They can't let a goal stop them from playing their best. They need to be ready for the next ball coming their way.

Goalkeepers have a great view of the field compared to their teammates. Field players move with the ball. But the goalie mostly stays in the goal area, which includes the penalty box. From this area, the goalkeeper can see the whole field. This allows them to have an idea of the other team's next move. They can call out instructions to teammates. They can help other players get where they need to be to defend or score.

There are three basic goalkeeping styles. They include sweeper keeper, line keeper, and ball-playing keeper. A sweeper keeper sometimes plays as another defender higher up on the field. Sweeper-keepers are good at one-on-one saves. A line keeper plays on the goal line. Line keepers are focused on watching the ball as it is kicked and stopping shots immediately. The ball-playing keeper has great ball handling skills and can pass well to the wings. Ball-playing keepers often receive backward passes from teammates.

Goalkeeping is sometimes the most physical job on the field. Goalies often charge directly into the action to stop the ball.

GOALIE SAFETY EQUIPMENT

Since goalies have a unique job, they wear special safety gear to protect them during dives, slides, and blocks. Goalkeepers wear a long-sleeved jersey to protect their arms when they dive to the ground. They also wear padded gloves to protect their hands from the sting of the ball. Some goalie gloves have plastic, foam, or metal shells, either inside or over the glove, to protect the keeper's fingers. Like field players, goalies wear **cleats** and shin guards. They also wear sliding shorts, which are often longer and tighter than regular shorts. These are also padded to keep a keeper's legs from getting hurt on a slide.

Gloves and padded shirts and shorts protect keepers from injury during saves.

It is important for goalkeepers to have **spatial awareness**. They need to know where their body is as it relates to the goal area. They also must be aware of other players. Sometimes the goal area gets really crowded with players trying to score, and with teammates trying to help the goalkeeper to defend the net. Keepers have to keep their eye on the ball at all times.

A beginner goalkeeper can get better with practice. They can work on skills alone or with a coach or teammate. Having someone throw or shoot the ball helps with movement, focus, and anticipating shot direction. This can also help with knowing when to jump or dive. Goalies can also work on foot skills on their own using cones and by practicing passes and punts. Many teams have a special goalkeeping coach, and most goalies attend a separate practice to work on their unique skills.

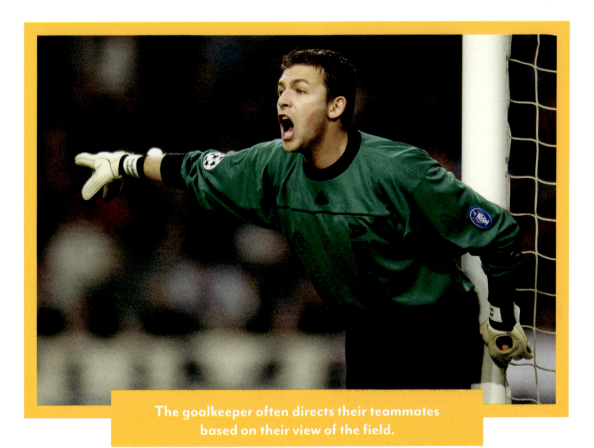

The goalkeeper often directs their teammates based on their view of the field.

CHAPTER THREE
GOALKEEPING LEGENDS

In the long history of soccer, a few goalkeepers stand out as great examples of how the position should be played. Italian goalkeeper Dino Zoff is one of soccer's most memorable players. He played for 22 years from 1961 to 1983, including 11 years with the Italian **club** team Juventus. Zoff was a level-headed player. His skills were consistent and cautious. He wasn't known for acrobatic saves. Instead of trying to show off, Zoff focused on the basics. Zoff was a strong and athletic keeper who was always focused on the ball. Zoff's ability to make quick decisions earned him a starting goalkeeper spot year after year.

One of Zoff's most memorable moments was the year before he retired. Zoff was the captain of Italy's men's national team at the 1982 World Cup in Spain. Italy was leading Brazil 3–2 with one minute left in the game. Zoff dove for the goal line to save a header goal. His save advanced Italy to the semifinal round where they defeated Poland. The Italian team went on to beat West Germany 3–1. Zoff was named Best Goalkeeper of the tournament.

Dino Zoff was 40 years old when he led Italy to victory in the 1982 World Cup. He is the oldest player in history to win the tournament.

Hope Solo started out as a forward and did not become a goalkeeper until she was in college. She scored 109 goals for her high school soccer team.

One of the most **decorated** goalkeepers in history is Hope Solo. She played for the USWNT from 2000 to 2016. During this time, Solo earned a World Cup title and two Olympic gold medals. Solo also received the World Cup Golden Glove award in 2011 and 2015. The Golden Glove is given to the most outstanding goalkeeper of the tournament.

Solo had many memorable saves. One of her best saves was during the 2008 Olympic gold medal game. The USWNT was playing Brazil, a top team. The game was tied 0–0 with 19 minutes left on the clock. Marta, one of the best soccer players in the world, moved around two defenders and took a shot. Solo watched the ball, raised her right arm, and stopped the ball with a dive. Team USA won the match 1–0.

Solo led the USWNT to 19 titles, including a World Cup win and two Olympic gold medals.

Many people consider Peter Schmeichel the best goalkeeper of all time. He led Manchester United to 15 titles during his 292 appearances for the team.

Peter Schmeichel is another legendary goalkeeper. He played for the English club team Manchester United during the 1990s. Schmeichel was known for his reflexes, shot-stopping ability, and leadership qualities. Standing 6 feet, 4 inches (1.9 meters), he was an intimidating force in the goal. His height gave him an advantage to reach tall and wide.

TIM HOWARD VS. BELGIUM, 2014 WORLD CUP

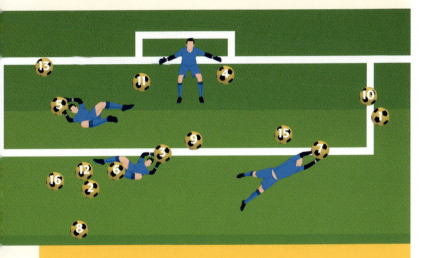

This diagram shows the location of all 16 of Tim Howard's record-breaking saves in the US's 2014 World Cup loss to Belgium.

A save that highlights Schmeichel's goalkeeping skills occurred in a match against West Ham United during the 1993–1994 season. West Ham had the ball. A player moved into the penalty box and took a strong shot on goal. The ball was moving fast toward the left corner. Schmeichel reached his arm over his head and sprung to the side just in time to swat the ball away. His save kept Manchester from losing. The game ended in a 2–2 tie.

SWEET 16

During the 2014 World Cup, United States Men's National Team (USMNT) goalkeeper Tim Howard made a record 16 saves in a single game. It was the tournament's Round of 16. The United States was playing Belgium. The losing team would head home, while the winning team would advance to the quarterfinals. Howard saved 12 goals with his chest and hands and four with his feet. He was an amazing example of how goalkeepers have to get creative to save the ball from going into the net. No goalie before or since has made 16 or more saves in a World Cup game.

CHAPTER FOUR

TODAY'S STAR KEEPERS

Soccer is more popular today than ever before. Some of the game's top keepers have played at multiple levels, from college to international competition. One of those goalies is Alyssa Naeher. She is a keeper for the USWNT. She is also the starting keeper for the Chicago Red Stars of the National Women's Soccer League (NWSL). Naeher began her career as an award-winning goalkeeper at Penn State University. She played for several club teams before joining the Red Stars in 2016. Naeher began playing for the USWNT in 2014.

In two separate tournaments during 2024, Alyssa Naeher made three saves and scored one goal herself during penalty shoot-outs.

She became the team's starting goalkeeper in 2016 after Hope Solo retired. In 2024, Naeher earned the Golden Glove award after the United States defeated Brazil to win the Women's Gold Cup tournament.

One of Naeher's most impressive moments was in April 2024 during a penalty shoot-out against Canada. Team USA played Canada in the final match of the SheBelieves Cup tournament. The game was tied 2–2 going into the shoot-out. Naeher saved one shot. Then, she stepped up and made a shot herself before saving two more. The USWNT won the match 5–4, making it their seventh SheBelieves title.

I'LL BUY THAT

One way fans show support for their favorite teams is by wearing player jerseys. Until recently, women's goalkeeper jerseys were not available for fans to purchase. During the 2023 Women's World Cup, fans of England's national team wanted to buy goalkeeper Mary Earps's jersey, but only field player jerseys were being sold online. Fans and keepers complained, and companies such as Nike listened. Now, women's goalkeeper jerseys are widely available, including NWSL goalie jerseys.

Brazilian goalie Alisson Becker plays for the English Premier League team Liverpool and for Brazil's men's national team. He joined the national team in 2015 and played in the 2018 and 2022 World Cup tournaments. Becker was named the Best FIFA Goalkeeper in 2019.

Becker played on several youth teams before joining his first **professional** team in 2013. He joined Liverpool in 2018. At the time Liverpool signed Becker, he was the most expensive goalkeeper in history. His **contract** with Liverpool was worth $84.7 million. At the end of Becker's first season, Liverpool advanced in the Champions League tournament. With Becker guarding the goal, Liverpool made it to the final round. They played another English team, Tottenham Hotspur, for the championship. Becker made several saves during the second half of the game to secure a victory for Liverpool. He had a total of eight saves during the match. For this amazing first season with the team, Becker earned the Golden Glove award.

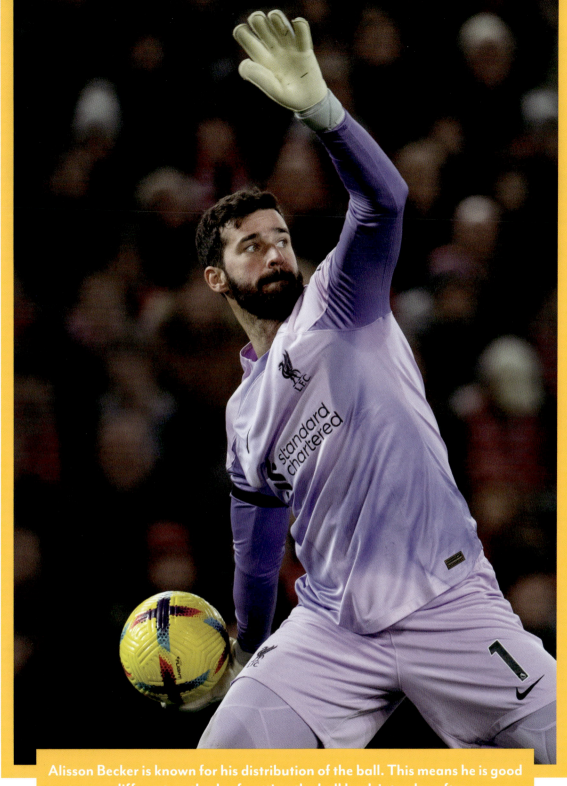

Alisson Becker is known for his distribution of the ball. This means he is good at many different methods of putting the ball back into play after a save.

Fans of Australia's national team nicknamed Mackenzie Arnold the "Brick Wall" and "Minister for Defense" after her performance in the 2023 Women's World Cup.

Mackenzie Arnold plays for West Ham United of the Women's Super League (WSL) in England. She became the team's captain in 2023. Arnold also plays for the Australian national team, known as the Matildas. Arnold played for several Australian club teams and in the NWSL for the Chicago Red Stars before joining West Ham United. She is known for being calm on the field. Arnold is a great example of a goalie who can keep her cool during an intense match.

One standout moment for Arnold was during the quarterfinal match of the 2023 Women's World Cup. The Matildas were up against France, one of the world's top teams. Arnold made nine saves. After 120 minutes, the game was tied 0–0 and went into a penalty shoot-out. Arnold saved three penalty shots, and Australia won 7–6. The Matildas advanced to the semifinal round for the first time in team history.

CHAPTER FIVE
RISING YOUNG STARS

As soccer becomes more competitive, goalkeepers must stay on top of the game. One young star who is making headlines is Belgian player Maarten Vandevoordt. Vandevoordt started his career with the Belgian team Genk when he was 17 years old. After an injury kept Genk's starting goalkeeper from playing, Vandevoordt got a chance to prove himself. He became one of Genk's starting keepers. As the team's top goalie for the 2021–2022 season, Vandevoordt kept 11 clean sheets. A clean sheet is when a goalkeeper stops all goals during a match.

Vandevoordt is considered a hidden gem because of his improvement over a short period of time. Early in his professional career, he was recognized as one of the best teenage soccer players in the world. He credits his Belgian youth team and training with Genk for his early success. He began as a field player and eventually began training as a goalkeeper. His time as a field player helped him understand the game from multiple angles. Vandevoordt joined the German team RB Leipzig at the start of the 2024 season.

Maarten Vandevoordt began playing in the Genk youth academy at the age of nine.

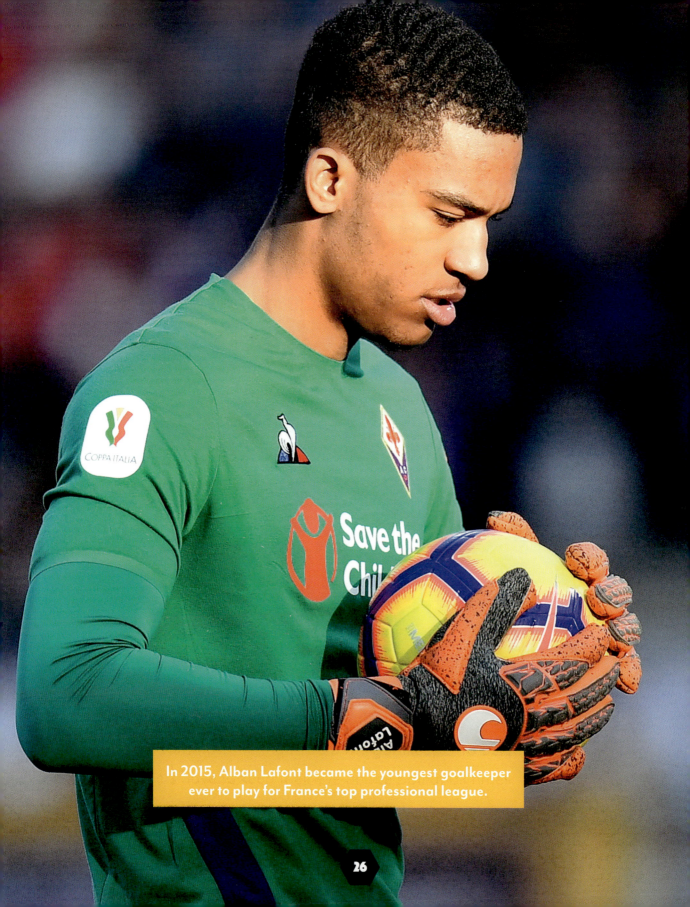

In 2015, Alban Lafont became the youngest goalkeeper ever to play for France's top professional league.

Alban Lafont is another rising star. He joined the French team Nantes in 2021. He also plays for the French national team. In 2018, he was named the world's second-most promising soccer player under the age of 20. Lafont has continued to prove himself in the goal.

For the 2023–2024 season, he had seven clean sheets for the 28 matches he played with Nantes. Lafont is a goalkeeper who extends his body to save the ball. In an opening match against the club team Nice, he slid with both feet to reach the ball for a save. He keeps his eye on the ball and is not afraid to use his body to make a stop. Diving back and forth is normal for Lafont. Not only does he stop the ball with his hands, but he also pushes it away or catches it. This ball control is one of his greatest skills.

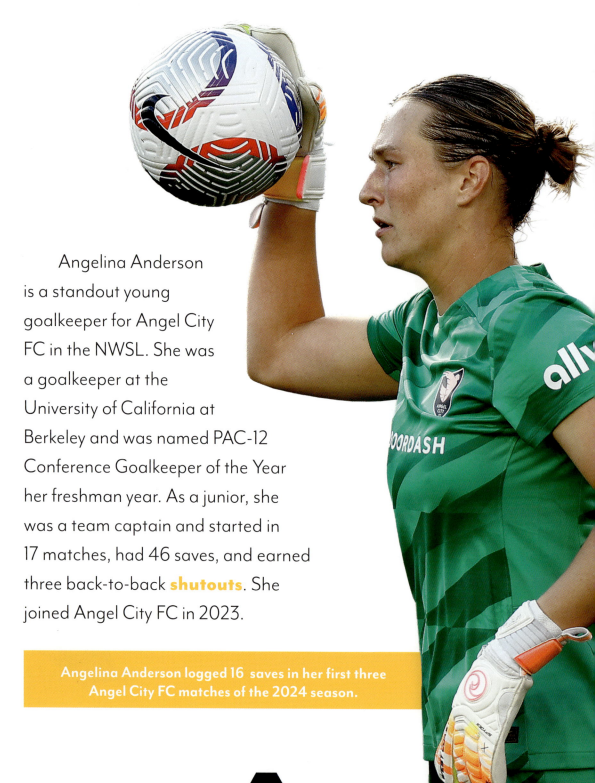

Angelina Anderson is a standout young goalkeeper for Angel City FC in the NWSL. She was a goalkeeper at the University of California at Berkeley and was named PAC-12 Conference Goalkeeper of the Year her freshman year. As a junior, she was a team captain and started in 17 matches, had 46 saves, and earned three back-to-back **shutouts**. She joined Angel City FC in 2023.

Angelina Anderson logged 16 saves in her first three Angel City FC matches of the 2024 season.

Early in her first season with the team, Anderson faced a penalty shot from Portland Thorns player Olivia Moultrie in the NWSL Challenge Cup. Angel City was winning 2–1 when Moultrie took the penalty kick. Anderson was ready. She fell to the right as the ball was kicked and it went right into her hands. Described as the hero of the match, Anderson helped her team keep their 2–1 lead for a victory.

Goalkeepers are the game's last line of defense. Sometimes they make one save that changes the game's outcome. And sometimes they make 16! From legendary keepers to rising stars, goalies are a unique and important part of soccer.

SAVE SOME, SCORE SOME

Sometimes a great goalie does more than defend the goal. In January 2012, goalkeeper Tim Howard played for the English club team Everton. In a 2012 match against Bolton, the score was tied 0–0. Howard received a pass from a teammate. He stepped up to clear the ball from inside his own goal area. His kick soared over both teams, bounced once, went over the other goalkeeper's head, bounced again, and went into the goal! It was Howard's first and only goal, and one of the most memorable in soccer history.

GLOSSARY

cleats (KLEETS) shoes with tiny spikes on the bottom

club (KLUB) a professional sports organization that pays athletes to play

contract (KON-trakt) a document stating the rules or terms of a business agreement

decorated (DEK-or-ay-tud) having won many awards, trophies, or medals

FIFA (FEE-fah) short for Fédération Internationale de Football Association; the group that oversees international soccer

handball (HAND-ball) a foul in soccer that is the result of the ball making contact with any part of a player's arm or hand

overtime (OH-vur-tym) time added on to the normal amount of playing time in a sports competition, used when a game's score is tied

penalty kick (PEN-ul-tee KIK) a free kick taken from the penalty spot inside the penalty box awarded when the defending team commits a foul inside the penalty box of their own team; only the goalie is allowed to defend a penalty kick

professional (pro-FESH-uh-nul) an athlete who is paid to play a sport

shots on goal (SHOTS ON GOAL) an attempt to score in soccer

shutout (SHUT-owt) a game in which the goalie stops every shot on goal and the other team does not score

spatial awareness (SPAY-shul uh-WAYR-nuss) understanding where your body is and how it is affected by other people or objects

FAST FACTS

- Italy's Gianluigi Buffon holds the record for most international appearances for a goalkeeper. He made 176 official appearances for his national team.

- Researchers say that goalies' brains might be able to merge signals from different senses more quickly, making their reaction time faster.

- The starting goalkeeper usually wears the number one jersey because they are the first in the lineup and are often considered the most important line of defense on the team.

- Only six goalkeepers in Premier League history have scored for their teams.

ONE STRIDE FURTHER

- Ask your friends and family if they have seen a penalty shoot-out in soccer. What made it exciting to watch?

- What do you think makes a great goalkeeper? Make a list of qualities.

- Review the skills listed for a goalkeeper. Which skill might be the hardest to practice and why?

- Now that you know more about goalkeeping, would you want to be a goalie? Why or why not?

FIND OUT MORE

IN THE LIBRARY

Lowe, Alexander. *G.O.A.T. Soccer Goalkeepers*. Minneapolis, MN: Lerner, 2022.

Miller, Spencer and Harrison Florio. *The Greatest Goalkeepers*. Surrey, United Kingdom: Paw Kingdom, 2022.

Walters, Meg. *World Cup Women*. New York, NY: Sky Pony, 2019.

ON THE WEB

Visit our website for links about goalkeepers:
childsworld.com/links

Note to Parents, Caregivers, Teachers, and Librarians: We routinely verify our web links to make sure they are safe and active sites. So encourage your readers to check them out!

INDEX

Angel City FC, 28–29

Belgium, 17

Chicago Red Stars, 18, 23
clean sheet, 24, 27

header, 12

league, 18, 20, 23, 26, 31
Liverpool, 20

Olympics, 14–15

penalty, 4, 6, 8, 17–19, 23, 29, 31

save, 4, 7–8, 10, 12, 15, 17–19, 20–21, 23, 27–29
Sweden, 4

USWNT, 4, 14–15, 18–19

West Ham United, 17, 23
World Cup, 4–5, 12–15, 17, 19, 20, 22–23